CLASSIC WEDDING SONGS

— PIANO LEVEL —
LATE INTERMEDIATE/EARLY ADVANCED

ISBN 978-0-634-07424-0

HAL•LEONARD®
CORPORATION
7777 W. BLUEMOUND RD. P.O. BOX 13819 MILWAUKEE, WI 53213

Visit Hal Leonard Online at
www.halleonard.com

Visit Phillip at
www.phillipkeveren.com

PREFACE

Finding the perfect wedding music can be both a joy and a challenge. This collection was assembled to help in that task. We combined traditional classical selections with classic hymn tunes to provide a variety of choices. Some of the settings were tailored to suit specific moments in a wedding ceremony. "Joyful, Joyful, We Adore Thee" was arranged with a processional in mind. "All Hail the Power of Jesus' Name" would serve well as a recessional. All will complement a ceremony with stately grace.

If you are searching for contemporary material, I would like to recommend the companion to this folio, *Contemporary Wedding Songs*. This collection features popular songs from a range of decades as well as some new, original contributions to the wedding canon.

Best Wishes,
Phillip Keveren

BIOGRAPHY

Phillip Keveren, a multi-talented keyboard artist and composer, has composed original works in a variety of genres from piano solo to symphonic orchestra. Mr. Keveren gives frequent concerts and workshops for teachers and their students in the United States, Canada, Europe, and Asia. Mr. Keveren holds a B.M. in composition from California State University Northridge and a M.M. in composition from the University of Southern California.

CONTENTS

AIR ON THE G STRING

By JOHANN SEBASTIAN BACH
Arranged by Phillip Keveren

Adagio

AVE MARIA
based on Prelude in C Major by J.S. Bach

By CHARLES GOUNOD
Arranged by Phillip Keveren

Andante con moto

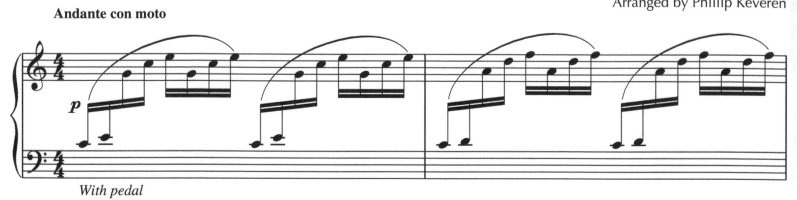

p

With pedal

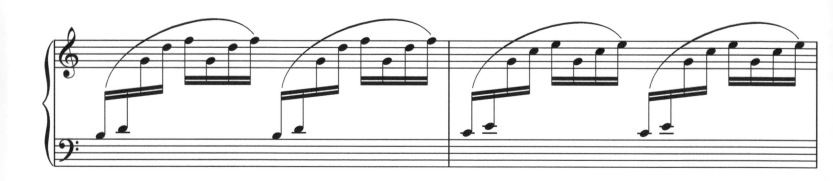

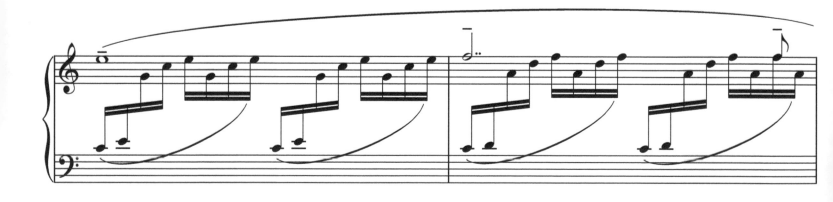

ALL HAIL THE POWER OF JESUS' NAME
(RECESSIONAL)

Words by EDWARD PERRONET
Altered by JOHN RIPPON
Music by OLIVER HOLDEN
Arranged by Phillip Keveren

Brightly

allargando

Maestoso

molto rit.

AVE MARIA

By FRANZ SCHUBERT
Arranged by Phillip Keveren

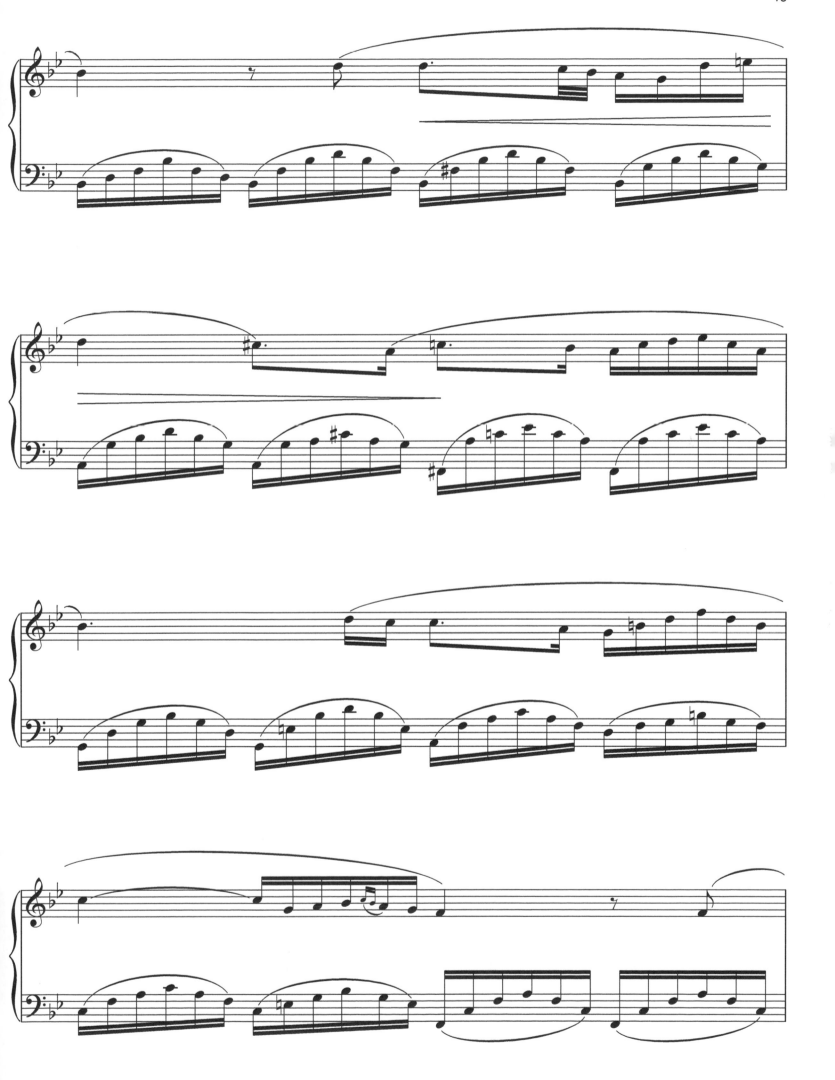

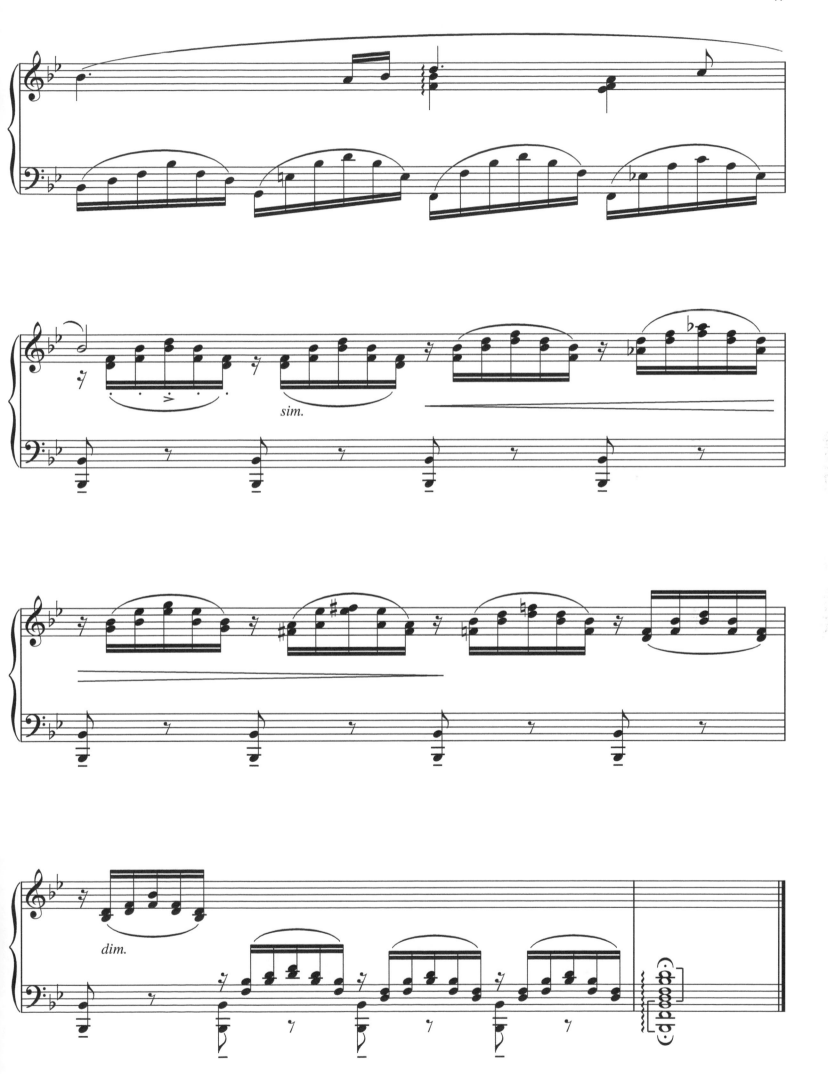

BRIDAL CHORUS

By RICHARD WAGNER
Arranged by Phillip Keveren

CANON IN D MAJOR

By JOHANN PACHELBEL
Arranged by Phillip Keveren

cresc. poco a poco

mf

JESU, JOY OF MAN'S DESIRING

By JOHANN SEBASTIAN BACH
Arranged by Phillip Keveren

MORNING HAS BROKEN

Traditional
Arranged by Phillip Keveren

JOYFUL, JOYFUL, WE ADORE THEE

Words by HENRY VAN DYKE
Music by LUDWIG VAN BEETHOVEN,
melody from Ninth Symphony
Adapted by EDWARD HODGES
Arranged by Phillip Keveren

O PERFECT LOVE

Words by DOROTHY FRANCES GURNEY
Music by JOSEPH BARNBY
Arranged by Phillip Keveren

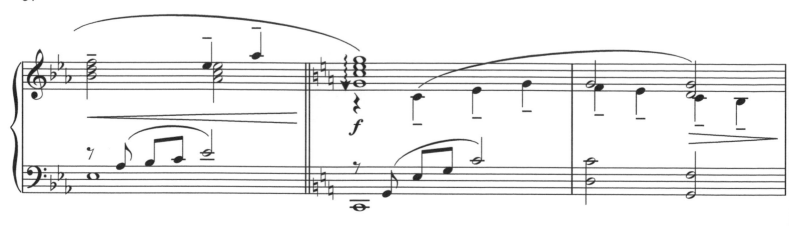

RONDEAU

By JEAN-JOSEPH MOURET
Arranged by Phillip Keveren

Allegro maestoso

SAVIOR, LIKE A SHEPHERD LEAD US

Words from *Hymns for the Young*
Attributed to DOROTHY A. THRUPP
Music by WILLIAM B. BRADBURY
Arranged by Phillip Keveren

WEDDING MARCH

By FELIX MENDELSSOHN
Arranged by Phillip Keveren

Allegro vivace

TRUMPET TUNE

By HENRY PURCELL
Arranged by Phillip Keveren

Stately

TRUMPET VOLUNTARY
(THE PRINCE OF DENMARK'S MARCH)

By JEREMIAH CLARKE
Arranged by Phillip Keveren

Allegro maestoso